Beautiful
north island
of new zealand

Beautiful north island *of new zealand*

REED

Published by Reed Books, a division of Reed Publishing (NZ) Ltd,
39 Rawene Rd, Birkenhead, Auckland. Associated companies,
branches and representatives throughout the world.

© 1997 Reed Publishing
ISBN 0 7900 0604 9

The authors assert their moral rights in the work.

All photographs by Holger Leue unless otherwise acknowledged.

Front Cover: Photograph by Stephen Robinson
Previous page: Opoutere Estuary, Coromandel Peninsula
Page 18-19: Auckland by Ian Baker
Back Cover: Kumara sign near Ruawai; L&P monument, Paeroa;
            Kiwifruit country, Te Puke

Designed by Sunny H. Yang

Printed by Everbest Printing Co.

Contents

The gateway to Auckland's Aotea
Centre, the work of Maori artist
Selwyn Muru.

Te Reinga to Auckland

T radition has it that Northland is where Kupe, the Maori discoverer of Aotearoa, landed. When he took the news back to the legendary Hawaiki it was of a place of sunshine, beauty and incredible potential. The east coast is a complex of deep harbours with names that roll off the tongue like breakers coming in from the sea — Parengarenga, Houhora, Kerikeri — down to Whangarei, the main city of the north. The west coast is a maze of estuaries and shallow harbours, dominated by the Hokianga Harbour. Everywhere there are long sandy beaches and small sun-baked settlements snoozing in the sun.

Once upon a time the rugged hills were totally covered with the kauri, King of Trees; although the majority were felled for the early shipbuilding industry there are still some stands remaining to remind us of the imposing forests that touched the sky. Other places are haunted with memories of the kauri gumlands, where Maori and Dalmatian worked together.

The Bay of Islands was the cradle of both Maori and Pakeha settlement and it was here that the Treaty of Waitangi was signed in 1840. From the grounds of the Treaty House you can look across to Paihia and Russell. Nearby Okiato was the site of New Zealand's first capital, although this was soon moved to Auckland.

Sprawled across the isthmus between the Manukau and Waitemata Harbours, Auckland has grown from a shantytown on the beach to become New Zealand's largest city, and the largest Polynesian city in the world.

Today Auckland is in fact four cities — Auckland City itself, North Shore City, Manukau City and Waitakere City. The centrepiece of Auckland City is Queen Street, which runs up from the harbour to Karangahape Road, but throughout there are suburbs of distinctive charm and individuality. The dance clubs and restaurants of Ponsonby, Herne Bay, Parnell, Mission Bay and Devonport are always busy, while the Polynesian markets of South Auckland are vibrant and alive.

Auckland's natural configuration is complicated by volcanic cones, the most dramatic of which is Rangitoto Island. More than any other feature, Rangitoto is a physical icon for Aucklanders, symbolising their love of the outdoors and their wonderful harbour.

Native flax provides a graphic
foreground to the Hokianga Harbour,
on Northland's west coast.

Kerikeri was the second Anglican
mission station in Aotearoa New
Zealand, and the Stone Store is the
oldest surviving stone building in the
country. Nearby are the beautiful
Rainbow Falls. Orchards abound near
Kerikeri, the country's premier citrus-
growing area.

Once a haven for tall whaling ships, the Bay of Islands is still a favourite destination of sailors, sunseekers and fishers. Cruises include the Fullers Mailboat, which delivers mail to the more isolated bays of the coast, and the fascinating Hole in the Rock. Later on, where better to relax than Russell's historic Duke of Marlborough Hotel?

The sundial on Russell's Flagstaff Hill overlooks the town and the superb Bay of Islands.

Pompallier House, which stands on Russell's waterfront, is now a museum illustrating the early days of Russell and the French mission which was based here under Bishop Pompallier. Traditional printing crafts are now undertaken here, recreating the mission's major activity last century.

The seagoing waka, or canoe, Nga Tokimatawhaorua, in the canoe house, Waitangi, and the interior of the meeting house on the grounds of the Treaty House at Waitangi.

Auckland is New Zealand's largest city. The Sky City
Tower is a dominant part of the skyline at 328 m,
taller than both the Eiffel Tower and the Centrepoint
Tower in Sydney. Sitting astride the Waitemata and
Manukau Harbours, Auckland is a boaters' paradise.

Built in 1929, Auckland's Civic Theatre is an architecturally elegant host to both movies and moviegoers. Further along Queen Street a pavement artist attracts a crowd who admire his work.

The city is connected to the North Shore
suburbs by the Harbour Bridge, built in
1959, with extra lanes added by Japanese
engineers (and wittily referred to as 'the
Nippon clip-on').

From the volcanic cone of Mt Eden the
island of Rangitoto provides a sculpted
backdrop to the city below. On the
waterfront, open air performers delight
visitors at any hour of the day or night,
while at Kelly Tarlton's Underwater
World spectators travel through
transparent tunnels within a giant
aquarium.

The life of the city. Chic Parnell owes its charm and character to Les Harvey, known to all as Mr Parnell. The Topp Twins are another Auckland institution; a singing duo, they really are twins. Just off Queen Street, Vulcan Lane provides an opportunity to rest one's legs, and perhaps enjoy a fragrant espresso or cappuccino in one of the area's fashionable coffee shops. In the Domain, the Wintergarden provides relaxation of a different kind.

The spectacular Marokopa Falls, near
Te Anga, in the Waikato.

Waikato to the Volcanic Plateau

During the Land Wars of the 1860s the Maori King Tawhiao threw his hat on a map of New Zealand and said, 'Where the hat lands I will protect all those who have given offence to the Queen of England.' The hat landed on the King Country, an area of limestone, which accounts for its often amazing topography of crags, ravines, canyons and caves. One such formation has become one of the great subterranean wonders of the world — the Waitomo Caves. The spectacular Glow-Worm Grotto shimmers with a million tiny lights like a miniature heaven.

The stronghold of the Maori Kings is in the Waikato on the Turangawaewae marae at Ngaruawahia. Not far away is Taupiri Mountain, where the Maori Kings are buried. Through this landscape winds the mighty Waikato River. Each year in March war canoes sail on the river as part of an annual celebration of Kingitanga, the heritage of the Maori King movement.

Right at the heart of the North Island is the Volcanic Plateau. The volcanic area actually runs from White Island on the east coast diagonally through Rotorua down to Taupo and the mountains of Tongariro National Park.

At Whakarewarewa Village, in Rotorua, Maori culture forms part of a theatrical backdrop of mudpools, hot springs, drifting steam and spouting geysers. If you want to be reminded of a more ferocious aspect of the area visit Waiotapu or the Waimangu Valley. In this region, in 1886, Mount Tarawera erupted, destroying the fabulous Pink and White Terraces. Drive on to Taupo, and when you swim in the lake, go yachting or fish for trout, just remember that once upon a time this was a volcano that blew its top.

28

A Maori sentinel stands to welcome visitors to the Ohaki Maori village on the approach to the Waitomo Caves.

At Waitomo, in the King Country, sightseers come from all over the world to visit the magnificent Waitomo Caves, one of the world's natural wonders. The traditional boat journey will take you through the caves, or you can join a blackwater rafting tour to explore this underground world in more adventurous fashion.

The city of Rotorua, with its ever-present smell of hydrogen sulphide, is at the heart of a region known for its spectacular volcanic beauty. Among its many attractions is the historic bathhouse in the Government Gardens, home of the Rotorua Art and History Museum. Also of interest is the Agrodome, which regularly features demonstrations of sheep shearing and

dog working. But Rotorua is not only a mecca for tourists; its setting enables locals to enjoy lakeside living beside one of the many lakes in the area.

Rotorua's Whakarewarewa Reserve is a
major centre of Maori culture and has
become an important school of learning
for Maori craftsmen and women. At its
entrance visitors practise the hongi, the
traditional Maori greeting. The carvings
on the meeting house have a special
significance for the local people.

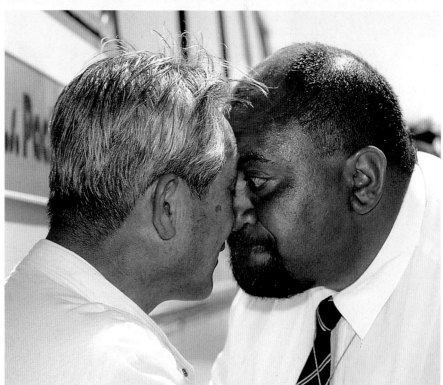

32

The Te Arawa people are well known for their spectacular singing and dancing. Women practise the art of poi dancing and men perform the haka. Traditional stories are told in the movements and actions that accompany the songs.

The area around Rotorua boasts an amazing variety of thermal activity. While the geysers and mudpools at Whakarewarewa (opposite, bottom) are well known, a visit to the Wairakei Thermal Valley (opposite, top) just 10 km north of Taupo can provide an equally dramatic experience of steam and bubbling mud. Halfway between Rotorua and Taupo the colourful Champagne Pool (above) is one of the attractions of Waiotapu Scenic Reserve.

Across Lake Tarawera can be seen the famous Mt Tarawera, which on 10 June 1886 exploded, destroying the fabulous Pink and White Terraces.

Steam rises from the Wairakei
geothermal power station, the second
largest in the world. The awesome
power of the earth's natural resources
can also be seen at the mighty Huka
Falls, on the Waikato River, a little
nearer Taupo.

New Zealanders and visitors from all over the world come to fish the waters of Lake Taupo and ski the slopes of Mt Ruapehu, whose warm crater lake looks deceptively quiet in the afternoon sun. Although the mountain has not erupted in recent times, it is still an active volcano. At the foot of the mountain stands The Grand Chateau, with Mt Ngauruhoe beyond.

Mt Ngauruhoe at sunrise, obscured by
the swirling clouds.

Late afternoon near Port Jackson,
Coromandel Peninsula.

Coromandel to the Wairarapa

Before the coming of the Pakeha, Coromandel provided an impenetrable screen of lush fern and kauri forest. Like the Northland forests, however, the kauri of Coromandel were soon felled for the ship-building industry. Gold was discovered at Thames and Waihi in 1867, and the gold industry flourished until early this century. Today gold is once again being mined at Waihi, but Coromandel is better known for the golden sand of its beaches and the wild beauty of its peninsula.

The shoreline of the Bay of Plenty can take your breath away, especially when pohutukawa blossoms in the summer. When Europeans settled the area it was developed into sheep and cattle country, but today oranges, kiwifruit and grapes have taken over. The harvest is shipped to markets around the world.

South of the Bay of Plenty is East Cape. For a time whaling flourished along the coast, but today's pursuits are primarily fishing, sheep and cattle grazing, and forestry. The settlements haven't changed much since the old days, resembling frontier towns out of a Western movie.

The beaches around the Cape, Poverty Bay and down through Hawke's Bay are among the most magnificent in New Zealand, and the whole coast resonates with history, both Maori and Pakeha. Some of the biggest Maori meeting houses are found here, and some of the North Island's most graceful colonial houses.

Inland from the Cape are the mysterious Ureweras, home of the Tuhoe people, the Children of the Mist. Their kingdom is a mountain fortress guarded by rocky terrain, silver waterfalls and lakes.

Hawke's Bay is the home of some of New Zealand's great sheep stations. More recently its climate has encouraged diversification into horticulture, market gardening and orcharding. Half of New Zealand's wine is made in Hawke's Bay. The twin cities of the area, Napier and Hastings, were severely damaged in an earthquake in 1931. Napier was reconstructed in the angular, jazzy, Art Deco style and today is known as the Art Deco Capital of the World.

Then there's the Wairarapa, the centre of New Zealand's Scandinavian community, and a strong agricultural region. The main city of the Wairarapa is Masterton, while nearby Martinborough is the centre of a growing wine industry.

The deserted peace of Cathedral Cove,
near Hahei, on the Coromandel
Peninsula, contrasts with the gentle
clamour of a livestock auction at nearby
Coroglen.

Driving Creek railway, the creation of
potter Barry Brickell, winds up through
the brilliant green of the bush to a view
across the Coromandel valley.

The east coast of the Coromandel Peninsula looks straight across the ocean to the place where the sun rises. Here at Opoutere the sunrises are dramatic, with colours ranging from delicate ochres and pinks to cerise, violet and vermillion.

The fishing boat *Gay Dolphin* tosses in Coromandel Harbour in a sea quickening with the tide. At Thames memories abound of the gold rushes of the 1860s and '70s, when the town's population reached 20,000, almost twice that of Auckland. The Brian Boru Hotel, one of the few remaining accommodation houses, is best known today for its Murder Mystery weekends.

White Island, in the Bay of Plenty,
occasionally sends up steam and lava
just to remind us that it is still an active

Mt Maunganui, famous for its surf, is a favourite summer holiday spot in the sunny Bay of Plenty.

On the wall of a fish and chip shop at Katikati, a family poses outside a typical Bay of Plenty church, as if waiting for a photograph to be taken. On the beach near Opotiki, two Maori seek the succulent pipi, a shellfish regarded as a delicacy.

The East Coast has a relaxed lifestyle,
and the drive around the coast is for
those with plenty of time, who are
happy to leave themselves open to
whatever happens next. The locals
usually have time for a friendly chat.
During cultural practice at Apanui
School, Te Kaha, a young girl grins with
enjoyment and fun, and boys try to
come to grips with the finer points of
the haka.

A dolphin leaps during a sea world display at Marineland, Napier, one of several attractions on the city's waterfront. Cape Kidnappers, a short drive from Napier, is home to a colony of about 5,000 gannets. Some people walk around the coast to the colony; others prefer to be driven all the way.

Castlepoint Lighthouse, east of
Masterton, signals a warning to ships off
the wild Wairarapa coast. A fishing boat
shelters in the lee of the headland.

Two trampers in Whanganui National
Park, near the Bridge to Nowhere.

Taranaki to Wellington

On a clear day, Taranaki (also known as Mt Egmont) can be seen from the South Island. It made itself known to the earliest Maori canoe voyagers but when Abel Tasman sailed past in 1642 it hid itself from him. However, for James Cook in 1770 Taranaki was kinder. He saw it through cloud and rain, with lightning dancing around its crown. In 1841 ships of the New Zealand Company arrived from England's Plymouth and, within the gaze of Taranaki, established the settlement of New Plymouth.

From the summit of Taranaki you feel as if you can see the world. Ruapehu, Taranaki's brother mountain, is eastward. Seaward is a curve of black sand, like a fin flicking at the deep blue of the Tasman Sea. Below, the rainforest carpets the flanks of the mountain, and beyond the plains roll towards New Plymouth and Hawera to the south. Offshore, oil rigs dot the Taranaki Bight.

To the south, the deep gorges, waterfalls and wilderness of the Whanganui River have a special attraction for those who would explore it by canoe, white-river raft or jetboat. The Rangitikei and Manawatu rivers, further inland, are just as stunning. At the seaward end of the Manawatu gorge is the largest city of the plains, Palmerston North. For many years a university town, today Palmerston North is also a centre for agricultural and horticultural research, and for wider education.

Wellington, the capital, is one of New Zealand's most cultured and vibrant cities. The suburbs of Wellington all retain their own special character. Newtown, for example, is a mix of Maori, Pacific Island, Greek and new immigrant families, creating a joyful blend of fun and excitement. In recent years the waterfront and inner city have been transformed into a showcase of art, music, theatre and culture. Innovative architecture has added a new and exciting look to the city, contrasting with the older, gentler areas of Mount Victoria and Tinakori Road.

Mt Taranaki, also known as Mt Egmont, is New Zealand's most climbed mountain and the centrepiece of Egmont National Park. The mountain is a volcanic cone, sculpted into its present shape by past eruptions. Below the steep upper slopes dark forest takes over, in turn giving way to the softer colours of the Taranaki farmland.

Whanganui National Park, which opened in 1987, encompasses 79,000 hectares of lowland forest on both sides of the Whanganui River. The Park is popular with trampers, many of whom head for the Bridge to Nowhere. Built in 1936, the bridge was never fully utilised as many settlers were abandoning the area by the time of its completion. Today the area's main industry is tourism, and the river provides exciting jet-boating and canoeing adventures.

69

Low sun illuminates Oriental Bay, one
of Wellington's most attractive suburbs.

Wellington's Beehive is an addition
to the old Parliament Buildings.
Opened in 1981, it was inspired, so
people say, by the logo on a box of
matches.

The Cable Car provides a swift,
steep ride from the inner city, seen
here from Tinakori Hill, to the
university suburb of Kelburn.

The Wellington skyline has been transformed in recent years, with a number of striking new buildings. Wellingtonians are particularly proud of their Civic Square, with its paved courtyard and tiled fountains. The metallic nikau palm is one of several that surround the Wellington City Library. The library's curvilinear glass walls reflect light from a tiled pool.

Unlawful parking in Wellington. A busker
earns his keep at Manners Mall.

The lights of Wellington shine bright in this view from Mount Victoria.

The InterIslander Ferry is one way to
travel between the North and South
Islands of New Zealand. Here the ferry
is near Point Jerningham in the
Wellington Harbour.

Acknowledgements

Thank you to the many New Zealanders who welcomed me to Aotearoa and made me feel at home.

And thank you, friends and fellow travellers, for the inspiration and the best of times. You know who you are.

— H.L.

Thanks to Montana Wines Ltd and Air New Zealand for travel assistance in the South Island, and to Holger Leue, Ian Watt, Susan Brierley, Chris Lipscombe and Alison Jacobs.

— W.I.